D0712304

3

4

**OFFICIALLY
DISCARDED**

HALLOWEEN

CRAFTS AND COOKBOOK

HALLOWEEN
CRAFTS and COOKBOOK

BY NANCY HATHAWAY

With Illustrations By Hannah Berman

HARVEY HOUSE • NEW YORK

Manufactured in the United States of America
ISBN 0-8178-6130-0

Library of Congress Card Catalogue No. 78-73748

Harvey House, Publishers
20 Waterside Plaza, New York, New York 10010
Published in Canada by Fitzhenry & Whiteside, Ltd., Toronto

Table of Contents

THE STORY OF HALLOWEEN

Halloween is the night of the spirits. The Celts, an ancient tribe who lived in Britain, believed in ghosts, goblins, demons, elves and trolls. On this night — the last of the Celtic year — all of these spirits were allowed to roam the earth and torment people.

The religious leaders of the Celts were called Druids. They helped the people ward off evil spirits. They carried torches and lit fires to scare away the demons. In Wales, they built bonfires on hilltops outside the village and the people danced around them with pitchforks. When the last flame died, they ran back to the village as fast as they could. They were afraid because they believed the devil would get the last person down from the hill.

Many people disguised themselves to look like spirits: They hoped a ghost wouldn't harm another ghost. To get on their good side, the people offered the spirits treats to eat. For protection, they carried sprigs of witch hazel and holly.

Superstitions are a part of Halloween. On this night, people believed they could tell the future by jumping over candlesticks. They thought children born on Halloween could see spirits and that if a girl washed her face in dew, she would become beautiful.

Pagan and Christian beliefs combined and have survived to the present. An Irish legend tells of a man named Jack. He couldn't get into heaven because he was a miser and he couldn't get into hell because he had played tricks on the devil. So he had to carry his lantern, carved from a turnip, over the earth until Judgment Day. Jack and his lantern are now remembered in our jack-o'-lanterns. Our costumes began with the disguises the Druids wore. Our tricks were once the pranks the spirits played on the frightened people. And our treats come from the goodies the Druids bribed the demons with. Halloween is a time when we can all become Druids again.

Cats were both sacred and scary to the Druids. They believed the animals once had been humans. Because of evil spirits, these humans had been changed into cats and now aided witches.

The Celtic festival was called *Samhain* (pronounced *SAH-win*), which meant "summer's end." Much later, when Christianity spread to England, *Samhain* became known as All Hallow's Even. They called it this because it was the eve of All Saints' or All Hallow's Day. This later became shortened to Halloween.

CRAFTS

HALLOWEEN COSTUMES

Dressing up as someone (or something) else is a basic part of Halloween. You could buy a costume, but making your own can be more fun. Everyone knows how to turn a white sheet into a ghost. Take that same sheet, tear it into strips, and wrap it around yourself; you can be a mummy! Or put a purple border on it, wear it draped around you like a toga, and you can be a citizen of ancient Rome. Can someone help you dye the sheet? A black sheet can be Dracula's cape or a witch's gown.

Scarves and earrings can make gypsy or pirate costumes. For the gypsy, add some beads. For the pirate, add an eye patch and a sword.

A silver foil helmet can be the beginning of a knight or a robot.

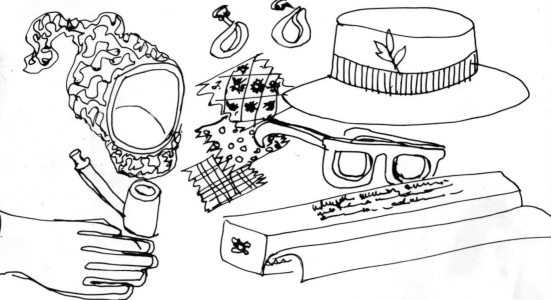

Sew some patches on clothes that are too big for you. Add a straw hat and a corncob pipe. You can be a scarecrow or a hobo.

Large cardboard cartons are useful. Climb inside a box so that you are wearing it around your middle. Add straps so it will hang from your shoulders. It can be a television set, a robot's body or a box of your favorite food.

Books, movies and television provide other ideas. You can be Wonder Woman, R2D2, Nancy Drew, Captain Hook, Amelia Earhart, King Arthur, Alice in Wonderland, Jesse James, Annie Oakley, The Cookie Monster, Pippi Longstocking, Huck Finn or an alien from outer space.

You can be an animal or a vegetable. Or, think about the things you enjoy doing, and dress up as a gymnast, a soccer player, a football star, a ballet dancer, a scuba diver, a magician or a jockey.

Paper Plate Masks

A green mask with long lumpy bags under the eyes and a third eye in the middle of your forehead can do a lot to improve a monster costume. Or cover your eyes with a red mask that has arching brows and a sprinkle of glitter. You can make these masks easily with paint and paper plates.

WHAT YOU NEED

paper plates
poster paints and brushes
string or yarn
pencil
scissors

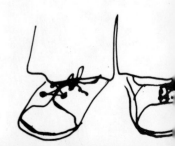

WHAT TO DO

Eye holes are the most important part of a mask. You can figure out where to put them this way: With your fingers, measure the distance between your eyes. Mark that distance in the middle of the paper plate. That is where the inside corners of the eyes should be. Draw circles or ovals for the eyes. Cut them out.

Now you're ready to design the mask. If you want a full face mask, cut a hole for the mouth (just in case you want to put something in it!). For an eye mask, draw the outlines of the mask and then cut it out. Now paint the mask.

When you're finished, punch a hole on each edge. Tie a string or a piece of yarn through each hole. Tie it behind your head. You're ready to trick or treat.

BEADS

If you are dressing up as an Indian, a movie star, a gypsy, a hippie or a rock-n'-roll singer, beads are just the thing to make your costume special. Here are two kinds of beads to make. You can make both kinds and then combine them.

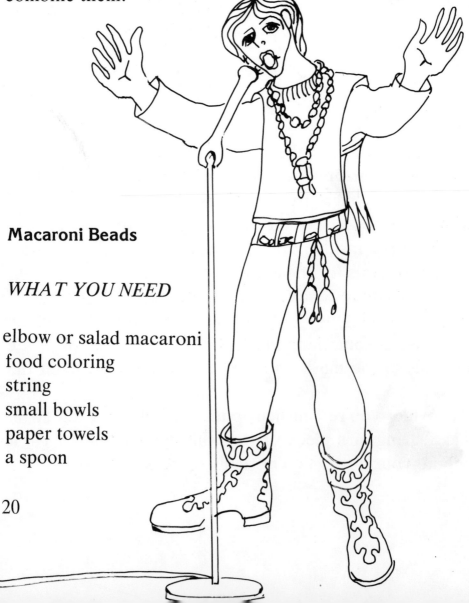

Macaroni Beads

WHAT YOU NEED

elbow or salad macaroni
food coloring
string
small bowls
paper towels
a spoon

WHAT TO DO

First spread newspaper over the counter. Food coloring sometimes splatters and stains.

Put one or two spoonfulls of dry macaroni into a small bowl. Sprinkle a few drops of food coloring over the beads. With a spoon, quickly stir the dye and the macaroni until the macaroni has turned color.

Spread the macaroni out on paper towels and let them dry.

Wash the bowl and spoon right away, dry them and start again with another color.

Remember: Red and yellow make orange. Blue and red make purple.

Paper Beads

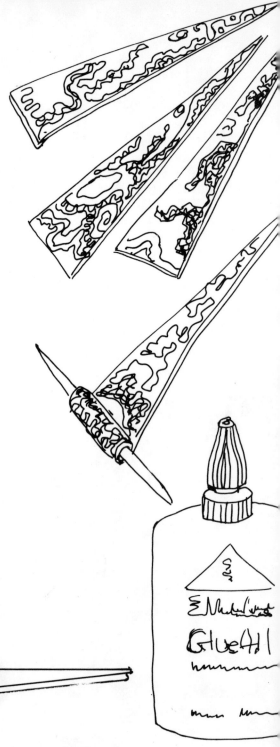

WHAT YOU NEED

colored paper
some old magazines
scissors
toothpicks
white glue
string

WHAT TO DO

Cut some long, skinny triangles of paper. They should be about five or six inches long and about one inch across at the bottom.

Begin to roll the thick part of the triangle around the toothpick. After you have rolled the paper just a little bit, put a drop of glue on the paper — a very small drop — and keep rolling.

Roll the paper tightly. When you are almost at the end, put another dab of glue on the paper. Finish rolling the paper and hold it in place for about half a minute in order for the glue to take.

Carefully slide the paper off the toothpick. You will have an oblong paper bead with a handy hole through the middle. If you used a magazine page, the bead will probably have a variety of colors on it in unexpected places. If you used construction paper, the bead will be a single color but it will be thicker than the magazine beads. A silver foil bead will be thin and elegant. Try all three kinds! When you string the beads, make sure you've cut enough string to fit over your head.

Halloween Mobile

Bobbing bats, swirling stars and a slowly turning witch can turn a bare branch into a Halloween mobile. With each puff of air, the mobile moves and every time you look at it, it's a little different. This mobile has a witch, a ghost, a jack-o'-lantern, an owl, a skull and stars.

WHAT YOU NEED

white tissue paper
construction paper
poster paints and brushes
needle and thread
tape
scissors
pencil
a branch from a tree

WHAT TO DO

Begin with the ghost. Crumple a small piece of tissue paper into a ball. This will be the inside of the head. Tie a larger piece of tissue paper around the ball with a piece of thread. Paint two eyes on the head. (Or use a felt-tip pen.) Take a needle strung with a long piece of thread knotted at the ends. Insert it up through the inside of the head. Pull the needle all the way through. Then cut off the thread near the needle. The ghost is ready to hang.

Paint the witch on a piece of construction paper or light cardboard. Give her a pointed hat and a long dress. She doesn't have to be ugly, though. You might want to put a rainbow over

25

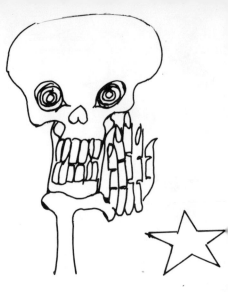

her head, or give her a cat, or a broomstick or a large bubbling pot to stir. When the paint is dry, turn it over and paint the back of the witch.

For the skull, paint white eye holes, nose hole and teeth on black construction paper. The owl can be any color you want. If you are not sure how to make any of these shapes, look at the drawing and use it for a pattern. Don't forget to make a front and a back for each piece.

Finally, make a moon and some stars. Use many colors for these. Silver foil and glitter add a nice touch.

Make a small hole at the top of each design and tie a long piece of thread through the hole. Tie each design to a different point on the branch. Some designs should hang a long way down. Others should have shorter threads. Make sure the mobile is balanced.

When each piece is tied to the branch, suspend the branch from the ceiling. Tie a double piece of thread to each end of the branch. Tape the thread to the ceiling. Your mobile will sway in the breeze.

If you cannot find a good branch, you can still make a mobile. Tape each piece to the ceiling. If you cluster the pieces together, they will look just like a mobile.

Finger Puppets

Finger puppets can be anything you like: a clown, a lion, an old man, a young girl, a shark, Queen Elizabeth or King Tut. Make a bunch of puppets. Then see if you can make up a play that has each puppet in it.

WHAT YOU NEED

felt
white glue
scissors
yarn, scraps of material, white cotton and anything else
you can think of.

WHAT TO DO

To make the body of the puppet, cut a rectangle out of felt. It should be three or four inches long and wide enough to fit around your finger. Glue one side of the felt to the other so that it forms a cylinder.

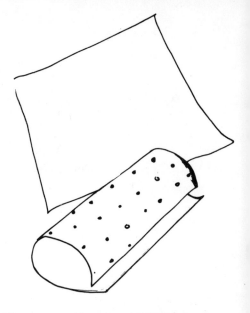

If you like, cut the head into a more rounded shape at the top. Glue the front and back together to form the head.

Now make a costume and a face. You might begin with a hat. The easiest kind of hat starts with a half circle. Fold it into a cone shape and glue one side of the cone to the other. You can use this pointed hat for a wizard, a clown or a magician. Cut the hat in half and glue the top edges together. This can be a fancy

spring hat, with ribbons and flowers, or a business hat. Upside down, with the longer edges glued together, it can be a crown or a sailor's cap. Put the hat on the body and glue it to the head.

Add a face. You can cut out eyes and a mouth from felt or paper. Or draw a face with a felt-tip pen. For hair, cut another piece of felt into fringe. You might add some yarn — maybe braided. Or use fluffy white cotton for an old person's hair.

Make the rest of the costume out of felt or scraps of printed material. Try adding a button, a feather or a small piece of yarn tied like a belt. Your puppet is complete.

Paper Stained Glass

Paper stained glass is easy to make and surprisingly beautiful. Put it in front of a window. When the light shines through the graceful swirls of color, the whole room will look lovelier.

WHAT YOU NEED

crayons

a plastic pencil sharpener

wax paper

an iron

scissors

tape

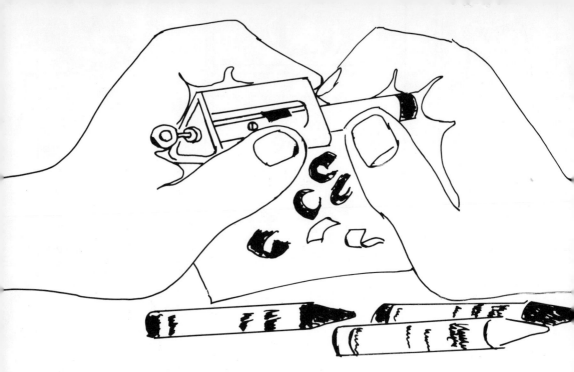

WHAT TO DO

Tear off a large sheet of wax paper. With the pencil sharpener, sharpen a crayon over the wax paper. As you sharpen, little curls of crayon wax will fall onto the paper. Leave them there, just as they fall. Add another one or two colors. Light colors look good with dark colors. The white crayon is pretty combined with any other color.

When the crayon shavings cover an area three or four inches across, tear off another large sheet of wax paper. Place it on top of the shavings. Gently pat the shavings. Carefully pick up the two sheets of wax paper and put them on the ironing board. Turn the iron to a low setting. It should be just barely warm. It may be a good idea to have a grown-up use the iron. Iron the wax paper over the crayon shavings. The crayon wax will melt, and the colors will flow into each other. The wax paper and the crayon bits will all stick together. Let it dry for a few minutes.

You can cut the paper stained glass in any shape you like. Simple shapes are best. Take a piece of tape. Form it into a circle, sticky side out. Stick this on the back of the shape. Then press it on the window. Or, hang it from a piece of thread in front of the window and watch it turn in the breeze.

These cut-out shapes are also pretty simply glued onto colored paper. You can use them for cards, invitations or bookmarks.

Placecards

Planning a party? You might want some placecards so everyone will know where to sit. Here's how to make them.

WHAT YOU NEED

construction paper
white glue
scissors

WHAT TO DO

For each placecard, cut a piece of paper about four inches on each side. Fold it in half.

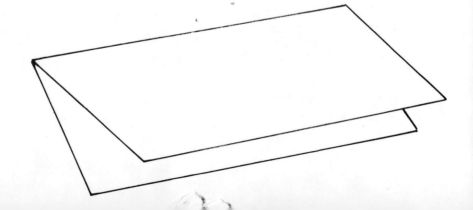

Make a paper cut-out using a different color. Cut any shape you want. One idea might be to cut out the shapes you see on playing cards — hearts, spades, diamonds and clubs. Or try pumpkins, flowers, stars or letters of the alphabet.

When you have cut out the shape, glue the bottom part of it to the front of the placecard. The top part will stick out above the fold. Finally, write the name on the placecard.

For variety, you can make placecards with pressed leaves, paper stained glass, scraps of material or glued-on macaroni beads. They will give the table a festive look.

Ghost Writing

Just because a piece of paper looks blank doesn't mean it has nothing written on it. If someone has sent a message in ghost's ink, all you have to do is hold it close to a lightbulb. Letters will begin to appear.

WHAT YOU NEED

milk or lemon juice
white paper
a toothpick

WHAT TO DO

To write the message, dip the toothpick into milk or lemon juice and write the words. When the "ink" dries (which will take a little while), the words will be as invisible as a ghost.

To read the message, hold it in front of a warm lightbulb for a few minutes. Gradually, the letters will darken and you will be able to read the message.

The Wizard's Code

When the bats are screeching through the darkness and even the toads are shivering, there's no telling who might be out. That's the time for using a secret code. Another time might be when you are sending a note in school.

Instead of letters, the Wizard's Code uses astrological symbols for the signs of the zodiac, planets and asteroids. Look at the code. Then see if you can decode the message.

♈	A	Aries		☽	N	Moon
♉	B	Taurus		☿	O	Mercury
♊	C	Gemini		♀	P	Venus
♋	D	Cancer		♂	Q	Mars
♌	E	Leo		♃	R	Jupiter
♍	F	Virgo		♄	S	Saturn
♎	G	Libra		♅	T	Uranus
♏	H	Scorpio		♆	U	Neptune
♐	I	Sagittarius		♇	V	Pluto
♑	J	Capricorn		⚳	W	Ceres
♒	K	Aquarius		⚴	X	Pallas
♓	L	Pisces		⚵	Y	Juno
☉	M	Sun		⚶	Z	Vesta

Hanging Masks

When we think of Halloween, we usually think of face masks. But there is another kind, too: masks to hang on a wall. You can make several and group them into an arrangement on your wall, or hang them one on top of the other for a totem pole effect. They will look like African or Indian masks.

This project will take two days to complete. On the first day, make a *papier-maché* form. *Papier-maché* (pronounced *paper ma-SHAY)* is a way of making a hard object out of paper and paste. One drawback to this is that it takes about twenty-four hours to dry. You will just have to wait. On the second day, when the mask is dry, you can paint it and hang it.

WHAT YOU NEED

newspaper
flour and water
     or
white glue mixed with a little water
a plastic container (such as the kind used to hold cottage
    chesse or yogurt)
one or more bowls — the bigger the better. (Wide shallow
    bowls are better than narrow deep bowls.)
poster paints
pencil
scissors with a sharp point
string
silver foil

WHAT TO DO

Turn a bowl upside down and cover completely with silver foil. Turn the edges of the foil under the bowl.

Tear newspapers into strips: some long narrow strips, maybe two inches wide, some short strips, some pieces about the size of your fist. Make sure you have plenty of paper.

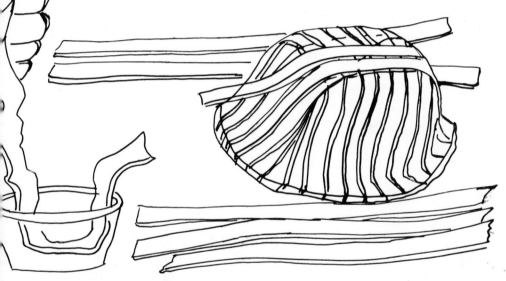

Make a paste out of flour and water. Put about half a cup of flour into the container. Add water until it is pasty but not watery. Or, you can mix white glue with a little water.

Take a strip of paper and smear it with the paste. The strip should be entirely covered with paste, especially on its edges. Press the strip on the silver foil.

Keep doing this until the bowl is completely covered. Be sure to overlap the strips. If the paste is watery, add more flour; if it gets too dry, add a little water.

When you have covered the bowl with about five or six layers of newspaper, you can stop. Make sure each spot, including the edges, is covered several times.

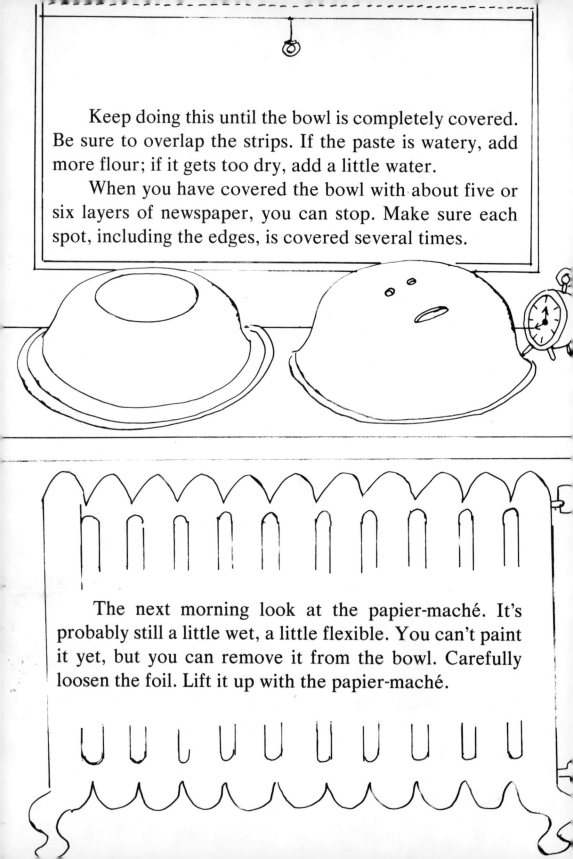

The next morning look at the papier-maché. It's probably still a little wet, a little flexible. You can't paint it yet, but you can remove it from the bowl. Carefully loosen the foil. Lift it up with the papier-maché.

Put the mask someplace where it can continue to dry easily. In a few hours, it will probably be dry.

Now you're ready to paint. Draw your design lightly with pencil on the mask. You might have used the kind of bowl that's flat on the bottom. That's OK. You can make it part of the design.

Paint the design. Cover the entire mask.

When the paint is dry, use the sharp tip of the scissors to make two small holes in the mask, one on each side. Make sure they are even with each other. Then, tie a piece of string through the holes and hang the mask.

Inkblot Cards

Inkblots are like clouds. If you look at them in a certain way, they seem to have pictures in them. You might see a butterfly, a rooster, an old tree or a crawling baby. Try making some Halloween Inkblot cards. You'll be surprised by what you'll see.

WHAT YOU NEED

white paper
construction paper
poster paints and brushes
white glue
scissors

WHAT TO DO

Fold a piece of construction paper in half. This will be the greeting card.

Cut a piece of white paper and fold it in half. Put a few drops of paint inside the fold. (If the paint is a little dry, add a drop or two of water.) Lightly press the paint through the paper. Unfold it. The paint will have formed a design that is the same on both sides of the fold. (The word for that is *symmetrical*.)

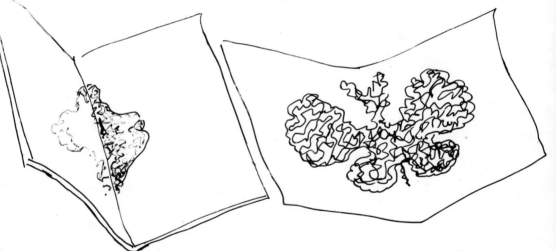

When the paint is dry, paste the design on the front of the card. Now write a message on the inside of the card. Make as many of these cards as you want. Like snowflakes, no two will ever be the same.

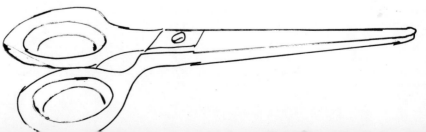

RECIPES

Ghostly Jello

This jello looks like little white ghosts are floating in it. It is a good addition to a Halloween lunch or dinner.

WHAT YOU NEED

1 package orange jello
1 cup boiling water   a pot
1 cup cold water   a spoon
1 8-ounce container plain yogurt   serving bowls for jello
 Optional: one small can mandarin oranges

WHAT TO DO

Boil a cup of water. Mix the jello with the hot water until it dissolves. Then add cold water.

Pour the jello into bowls. Take a big spoonful of yogurt for each serving and stir it into each bowl of jello. Some of it will dissolve a little, leaving ghostly trails in the jello. Some of it will stay in clumps, like the head of a ghost. You can also add mandarin oranges or fruit cocktail.

Chill.

Hot Apple Cider

Take a few sips of hot apple cider. Its sweet and spicy taste will warm you from the inside out.

WHAT YOU NEED

1 quart of apple juice (4 cups)
4 sticks of cinnamon
8 cloves
a pot
4 cups

WHAT TO DO

Put all the ingredients into a pot. Simmer slowly over low heat until the cider is hot and steamy. Pour the juice into cups. Do not put the cloves in the cups, but a cinnamon stick in each cup is a nice touch. Serves four people.

Gingerbread Jack-o'-Lanterns

These delicious cookies can be made into any shape you want. Decorate them with raisins, nuts and candies.

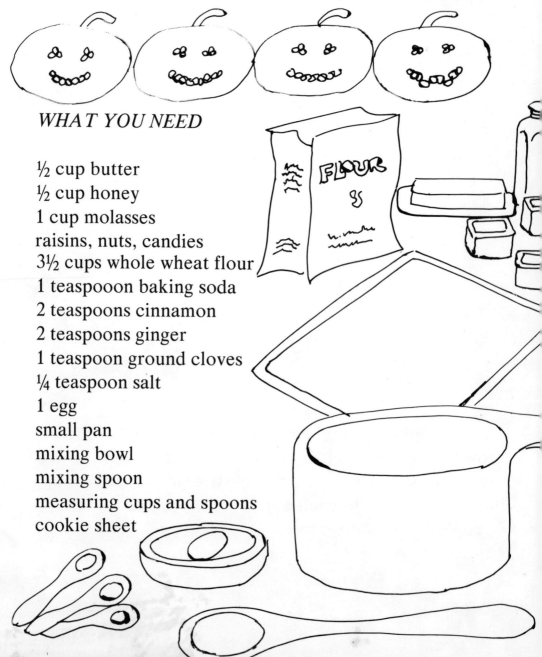

WHAT YOU NEED

½ cup butter
½ cup honey
1 cup molasses
raisins, nuts, candies
3½ cups whole wheat flour
1 teaspooon baking soda
2 teaspoons cinnamon
2 teaspoons ginger
1 teaspoon ground cloves
¼ teaspoon salt
1 egg
small pan
mixing bowl
mixing spoon
measuring cups and spoons
cookie sheet

WHAT TO DO

Measure the correct amounts of butter, honey and molasses. Heat the mixture carefully in a pan, until the butter melts. Then let cool.

While the mixture is cooling, measure the flour, soda, spices and salt. Mix in a bowl until the spices are evenly distributed throughout the flour.

When the molasses mixture has cooled off a bit, add an egg to it and mix well.

Pour the molasses-egg mixture into the flour mixture. Mix well.

Turn the oven to 350°. Then put the batter in the freezer for about ten minutes.

51

After ten minutes, the batter will be easy to shape. Form balls of dough the size of a quarter. Put them on a lightly-buttered cookie sheet. Flatten them until they are about ¼-inch thick. Attach a small piece of dough to the circle so that it will look like the stem of the jack-o'-lantern. Decorate.

You may want to try other shapes besides the jack-o'-lantern. It is easy to do this with cold dough. Sprinkle a little flour on a cutting board. Roll the batter and cut into any shape you like.

Bake for ten minutes at 350°.

Spicy Baked Fruit Slices

Here's a side dish that's delicious and healthy and goes with just about anything.

WHAT YOU NEED

3 apples
2 pears
a handful of raisins
1 tablespoon honey
1 tablespoon butter
1 teaspoon water
cinnamon
ground cloves

a covered baking dish
a knife

WHAT TO DO

Turn the oven to 400°.

Cut the apples into slices about ¼-inch thick. Throw away the core of the apple. Cut the pears into sections about ½-inch thick. Throw away the core of the pears, too.

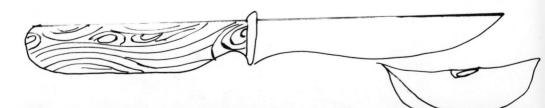

Grease the baking dish with a little butter. Put in a layer of apple and pear slices. Sprinkle with cinnamon, a tiny bit of cloves and raisins. Keep doing this until you have used all the fruit.

Mix the honey and water together and pour over the top. Cut the butter into small pieces and dot the top of the fruit with it. Cover. Bake at 400° for about 40 minutes.

Serve hot or cold, plain or with cream.

Peanut Pudding

For a new dessert, plop a dollop of peanut butter into a pot of pudding. Peanut pudding pleases people at a party.

WHAT YOU NEED

1 package vanilla pudding (the kind you cook — not the
      instant kind)
2½ cups milk
½ cup peanut butter
one pot
one large spoon
4 or 5 serving bowls

WHAT TO DO

Pour the milk into a pot and cook over medium heat. Gradually add the contents of the pudding box. Add the peanut butter. Keep stirring. As the milk gets hot, the peanut butter will melt. When the mixture begins to boil, it is ready. Pour it into the bowls. Serve it plain, or with whipped-cream or ice cream. It is good hot or cold. Serves four or five people.

Pumpkin Seed Snack

When you make a jack-o'-lantern, don't throw out the pumpkin seeds. Save them! Just a little bit of cooking turns them into a healthy and satisfying snack.

WHAT YOU NEED

a pumpkin
1 tablespoon cooking oil
salt
paper towels

a cookie sheet
a bowl
a spoon

WHAT TO DO

Scoop the seeds and membranes from inside the pumpkin. The seeds will be stuck in the membrane. Pull each seed out. Throw away the membrane.

Wash the seeds in water. Spread them on paper towels and put them in a warm place to dry overnight. When they are dry, shake them into a mixing bowl. Add one tablespoon cooking oil. Toss until the seeds are very lightly coated.

Spread the seeds out on a cookie sheet in a single layer. Lightly salt them. Bake for 15 minutes at 350°.

If you have some raw sunflower seeds, you can cook these with the pumpkin seeds, or just mix them up together afterwards. Pumpkin seeds are also tasty mixed with raisins or nuts.

58

The Ghoul's Graveyard

A bagful of brains. A wet, severed hand. A couple of loose, cold eyes. These things are part of the spookiest game ever — the Ghoul's Graveyard.

This game involves some preparation before your guests arrive. Gather as many of the things on this list as you can. You do not need all of them. Some of the things on the list may not seem very spooky. But when you touch them in the dark on Halloween, you may change your mind! Each thing will feel like a different part of the body.

59

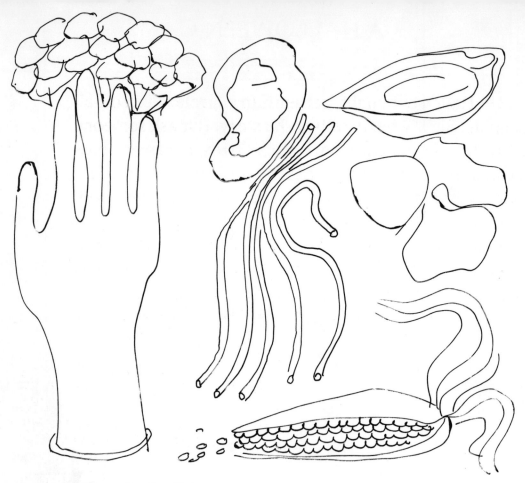

Here is the list:
a rubber glove filled with wet sand — a human hand
a dried apricot — an ear
a cold oyster — the pancreas
a piece of liver — just what it sounds like
cold, cooked spaghetti — intestines
a few hard kernels of corn — teeth
cornsilk — hair
a whole, cooked, greased cauliflower — the ghoul's
brain

On Halloween night, gather into a circle. Turn off all the lights. Slowly begin telling the story. (Or ask someone else to tell it.) As each part of the body is named, pass that item around in a bag. Let each person in the circle touch the pretend part before the story is continued. Each thing will feel weirdly real.

Before you tell the story, ask someone you trust to help you in another room. While waiting, that person might make a few spooky sounds. When it is time for the music, ask your helper to play a record at a speed that is too slow. When it is time for the monster to approach, ask your helper to stumble slowly into the room and breathe heavily.

Here is the story.

A long time ago, when a few scientists were putting together the Frankenstein monster, they had to find all the different parts. It was a long, slow search. Whenever there was a full moon, or on Halloween, they would sneak into a graveyard and look for parts. The first corpse they found wasn't much good — but they did get a hand from it. (Pass around the rubber glove filled with sand.) The next one provided an ear. (Pass the apricot.) Then came a liver, some intestines, the pancreas, teeth, hair and eyes. (Pass those, too.) With each new part, the monster just lay there, dumb. But at last, the brains were added. (Pass the cauliflower.) The monster slowly came alive. The first thing he did was to listen to some music. (Your helper will put on the record.) The monster loved music, but music made him hungry. So he began to search for something, or someone, to eat. He smelled something good. Slowly, he walked into the room, following the delicious smell. (Listen to the footsteps!) He pushed open the door. He took a deep, satisfying breath. And then . . . he turned on the lights!

And that is when you serve refreshments.

ABOUT THE AUTHOR

Nancy Hathaway writes fiction and articles and is the author of *Thanksgiving Crafts and Cookbook*. A former teacher, she lives in Venice, California.

ABOUT THE ILLUSTRATOR

Hannah Berman is an artist and teacher in the New York City school system. An exhibiting painter, Ms. Berman is the mother of two children and the illustrator of *Thanksgiving Crafts and Cookbook*.